Thank You Love
for helping + encouraging me

Many Paths

by Matthew Cory

The inspiration for this project came at an art gallery called the "Artic Raven" in Friday Harbor, WA. The graphic nature of the Native American art featured there struck me in a new way that day. Growing up in the Pacific Northwest, the very stylized art of the Natives from the region was always around, from totem poles to logos for local sports teams. But the way each piece in the gallery wove story and symbol, visual and spiritual, it jumped in my brain and took hold.

The pieces I created for this book represent being exposed to all spiritual thought at once, past and present merging in this information age. We are a culture that has access to immense amounts of knowledge and still feels lost and isolated. I believe everyone and every culture contributes bits of truth to the cosmic whole with their stories of how and why we are here. Be it myth or fact, the lessons and inspiration are still there. I looked for stories, characters and symbols within the world's religions that had something in common, a shared ideal or lesson, or miraculous event, anything that had a link to another culture's thought. Although each has a unique and varied tradition, I started to notice the similarities between the artistic expression of each religion and culture as well. Patterns and colors. Gods and teachers. Language and symbols. Images and thoughts began to fill my sketch book. I filtered it all through the lens of what I had seen that day in the gallery. Two years later, this is the outcome.

As Carl Jung suggested, an image or symbol carries some kind of intangible meaning with it whether or not the intent or original meaning was felt or expressed. Each image is accompanied by one or more quotes from Native Americans that speak to my feelings behind the work and what I've come to believe. My intent here is not to tell you the whole story of Spirit or what exactly it means to me or "should" mean to you, but to intrigue you enough that you might go searching for the answers and find yourself along the way.

Thank you for taking the time,
Matthew Cory

"Wakan Tanka, Great Spirit, Great Mystery, teach me how to trust my heart, my mind, my intuition, my inner knowing, the senses of my body, the blessings of my spirit. Teach me to trust these things so that I may enter my Sacred Space and love beyond my fear, and thus walk in balance with the passing of each glorious sun."
                                            - Lakota Prayer

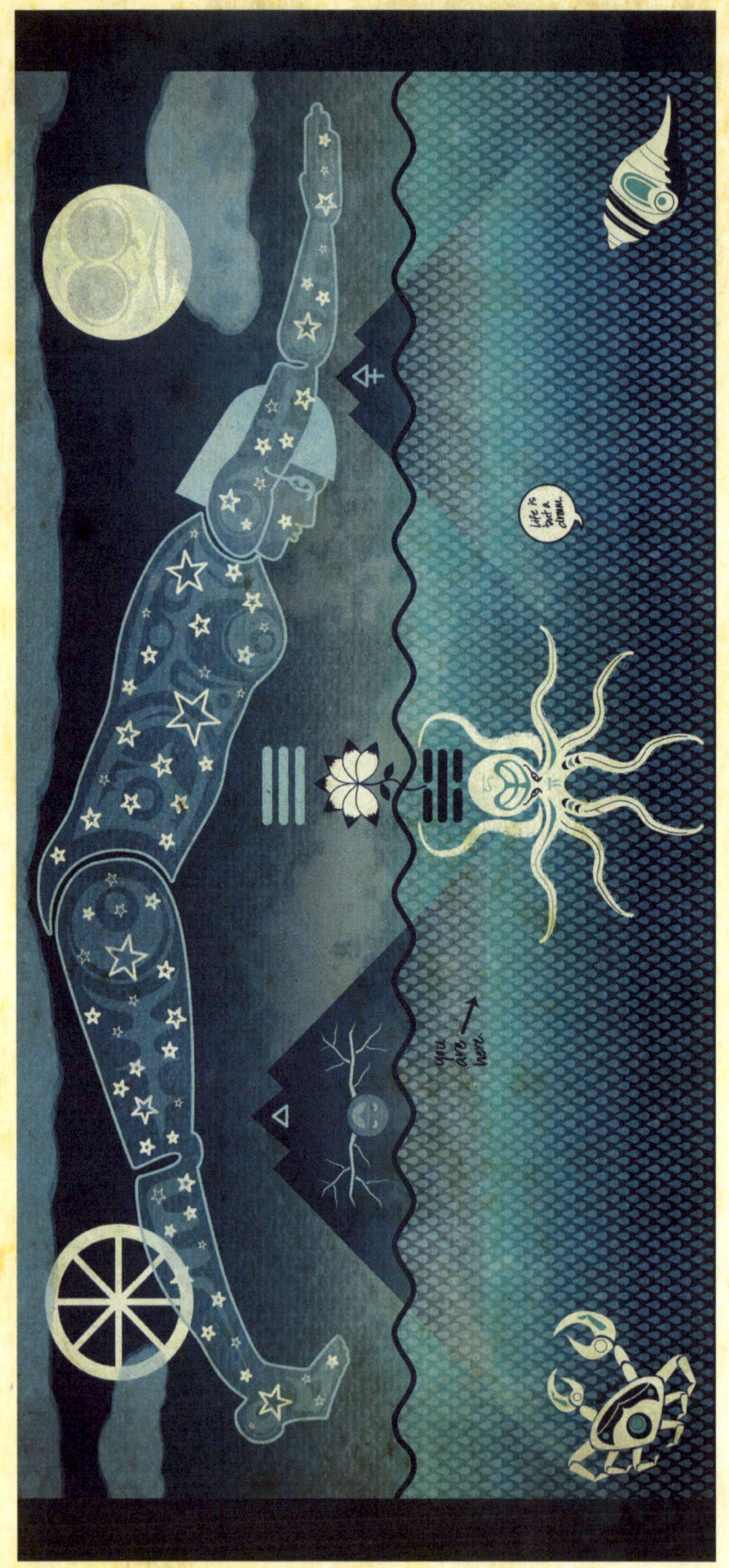

Illusion

"Humankind has not woven the web of life.
We are but one thread within it.
Whatever we do to the web, we do to ourselves.
All things are bound together.
All things connect."

— Chief Seattle (Sealth)

"Sometimes I go about pitying myself
And all the while I am being carried across
The sky by beautiful clouds."

— Ojibway Indian Poem

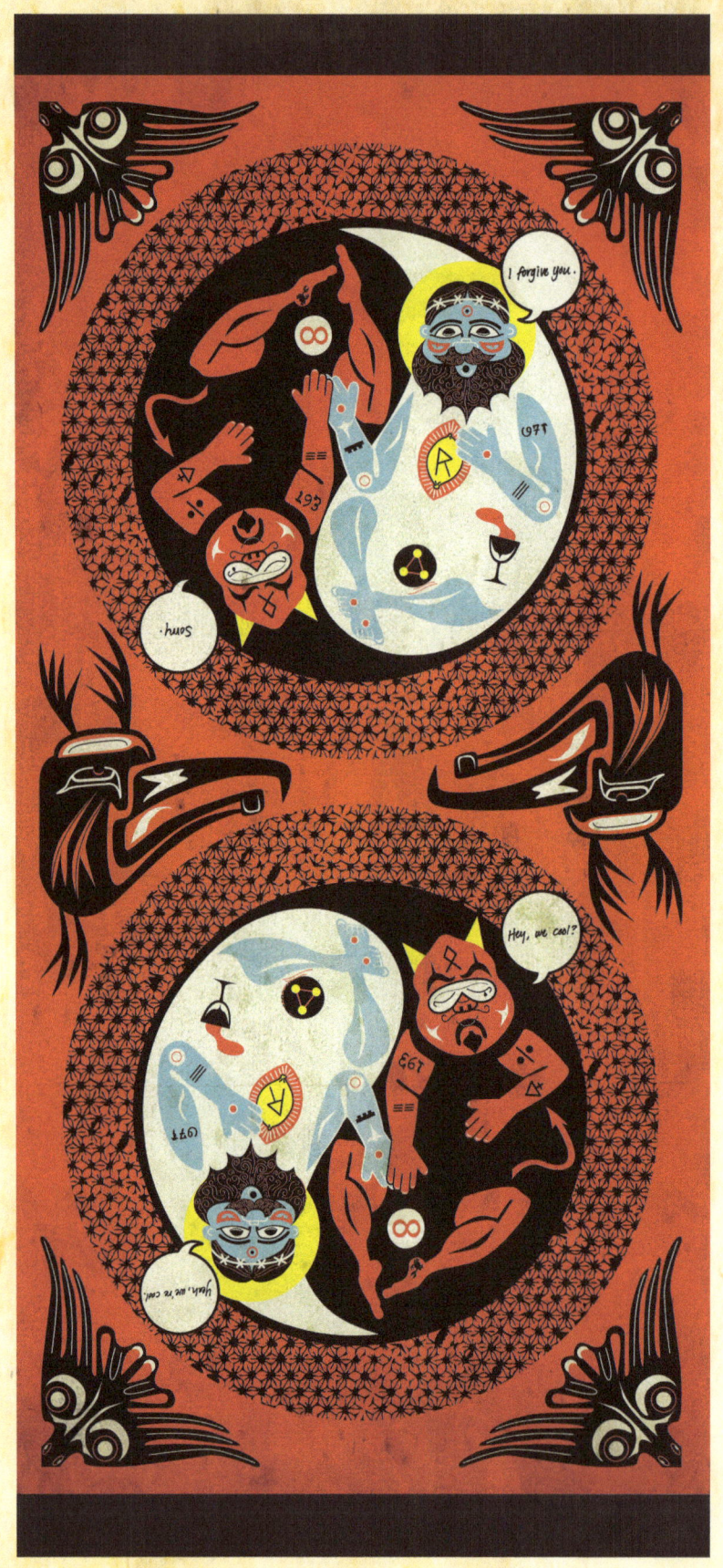

Duality

"All things in the world are two. In our minds we are two,
good and evil. With our eyes we see two things, things that
are fair and things that are ugly.... We have the right hand
that strikes and makes for evil, and we have the left hand
full of kindness, near the heart. One foot may lead us to
an evil way, the other foot may lead us to a good.
So are all things two, all two."
 - Eagle Chief (Letakos-Lesa) Pawnee

"Two worlds exist. The Seen World and the Unseen World.
Sometimes these worlds are called the Physical World and
the Spiritual World. The Elders say, when it is time to go
to the other side, our relatives will appear a few days
before to help us enter the Spirit World. This is a happy
place; the hunting is good; the place of the grandfathers,
the Creator, the Great Spirit, God, is a joyful place."
 - Nez Perce

"Dissimilar things were fitted together to make
something beautiful and whole."
 -Nippawanock, Arapahoe

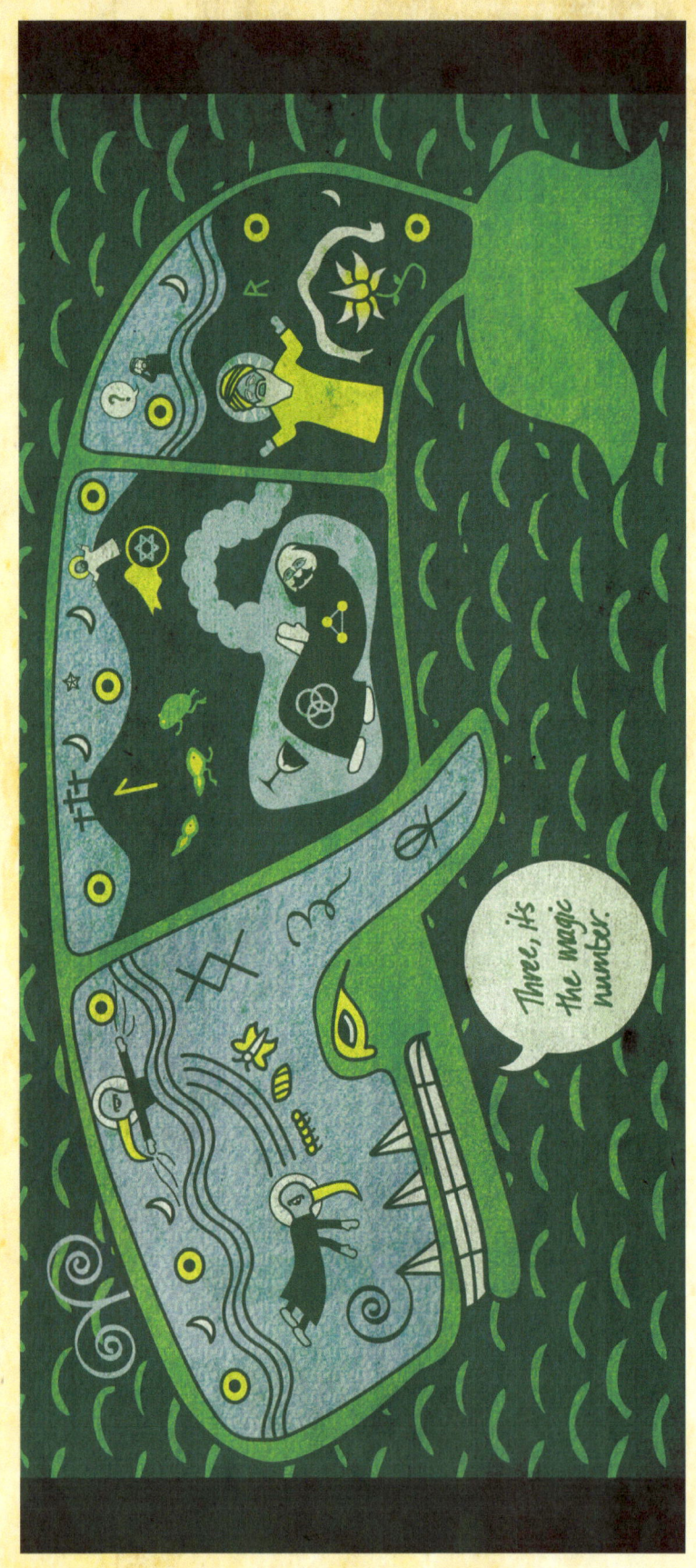

Energy Flows + Continues

"When you know who you are;
when your mission is clear and you
burn with the inner fire of unbreakable will;
no cold can touch your heart;
no deluge can dampen your purpose.
You know that you are alive."

— Chief Seattle (Sealth)

"What is life? It is the flash of a firefly in the night.
It is the breath of a buffalo in the wintertime.
It is the little shadow which runs across the grass
and loses itself in the sunset."

— Crowfoot, Blackfoot

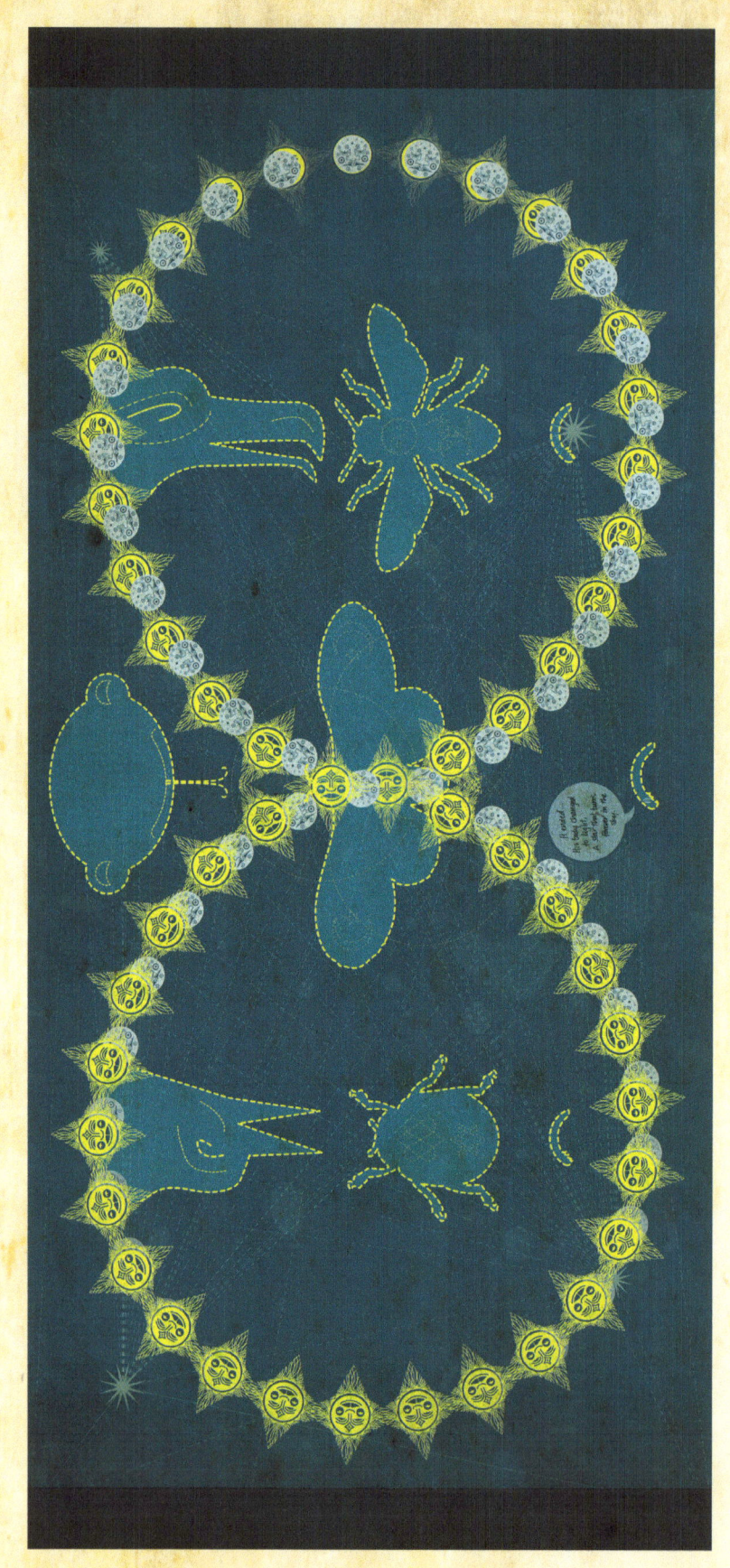

Phases

"The growing and dying of the moon reminds us of
our ignorance which comes and goes- but when the
moon is full it is as if the Great Spirit were upon
the whole world.

— Black Elk, Oglala Sioux

"If you listen close at night, you will hear the creatures
of the dark, all of them sacred – the owls, the crickets,
the frogs, the nightbirds – and you will hear beautiful songs,
songs you have never heard before. Listen with your heart.
Never stop listening."

–Henery Quick Bear, Lakota

"May the stars carry your sadness away,
May the flowers fill your heart with beauty,
May hope forever wipe away your tears,
And, above all, may silence make you strong."

– Chief Dan George

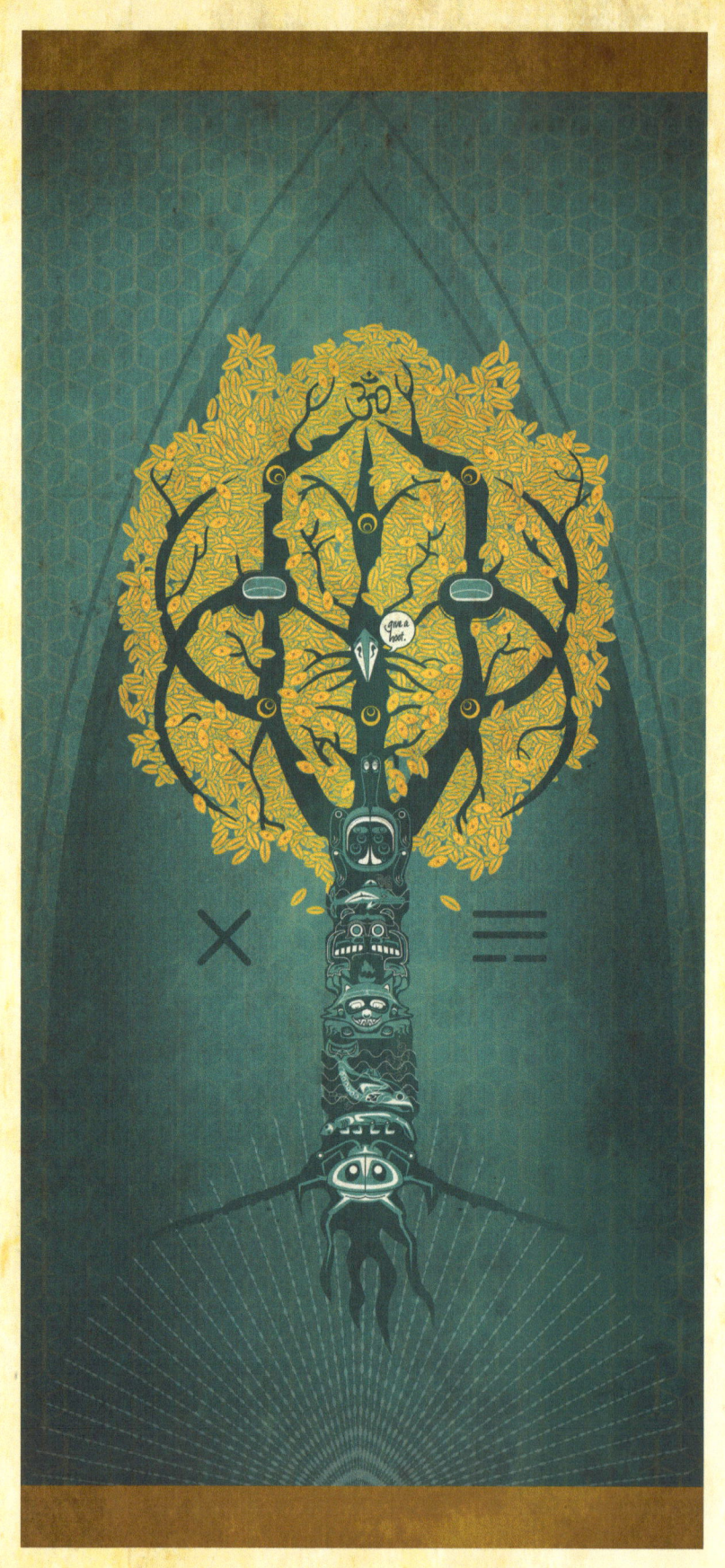

Tree of Life

"In the beginning of all things, wisdom and knowledge
were with the animals, for Tirawa, the One Above, did
not speak directly to man. He sent certain animals to
tell men that he showed himself through the beast, and
that from them, and from the stars and the sun and moon
should man learn.. all things tell of Tirawa."
   - Eagle Chief (Letakos-Lesa), Pawnee

"We all come from the same root,
but the leaves are all different."
   - John Fire Lame Deer, Lakota

"The Great Spirit is in all things, he is in the air
we breathe. The Great Spirit is our Father, but
the Earth is our Mother. She nourishes us, that which
we put into the ground she returns to us."
   - Big Thunder (Bedagi) Wabanaki Algonquin

"A wee child toddling in a wonder world, I prefer to their
dogma my excursions into the natural gardens where the
voice of the Great Spirit is heard in the twittering of birds,
the rippling of mighty waters, and the sweet breathing of
flowers. If this is Paganism, then at present, at least,
I am a Pagan."
   - Zitkala-Sa

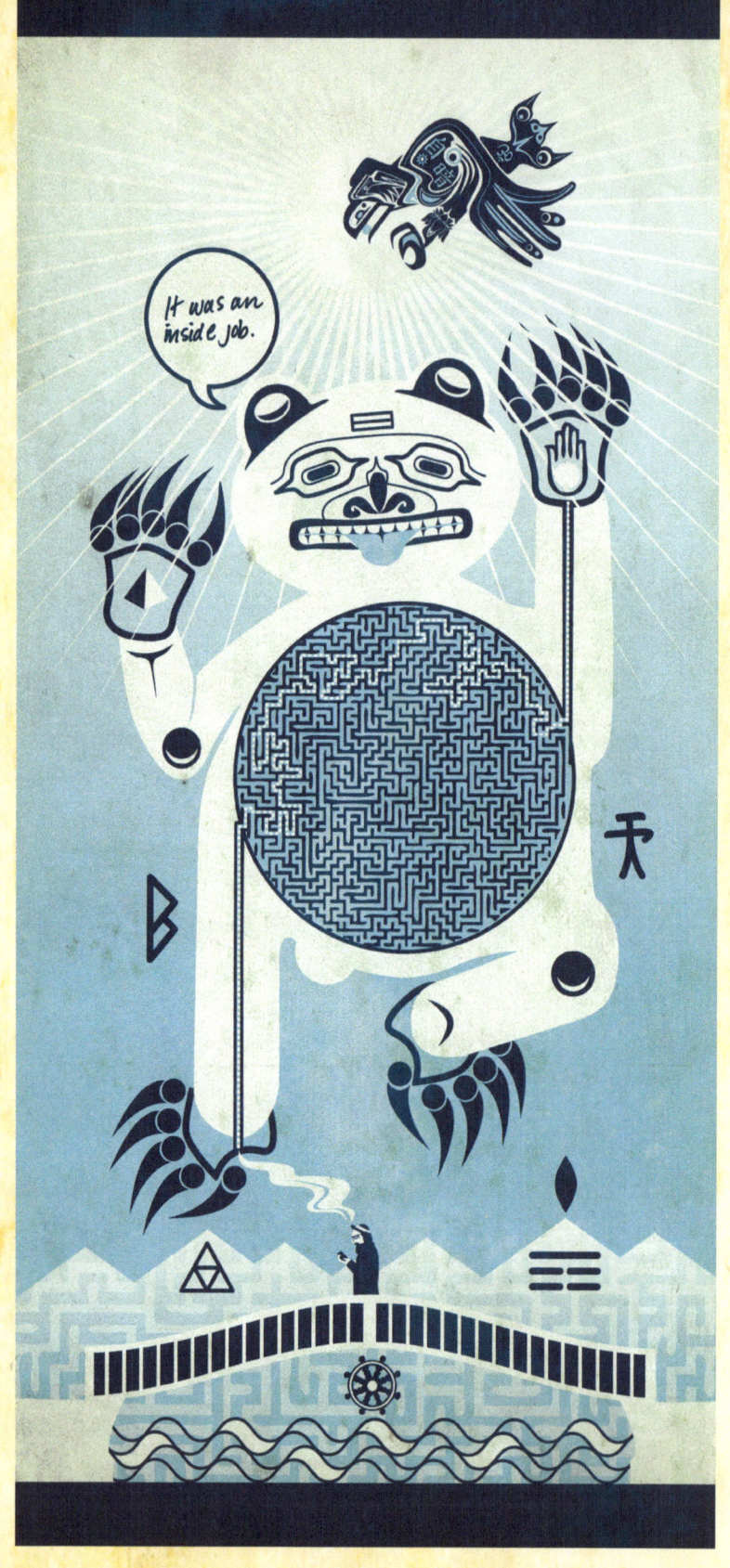

Search

"I have seen that in any great undertaking it is
not enough for a man to depend simply upon himself."
    - Lone Man (Isna-la-wica), Teton Sioux

"Without a sacred center, no one knows right from wrong."
    - Thomas Yellowtail, Crow

"The Raven's Tale.
Long ago no divisions existed between humans, animals
and spirits. All things of the earth, sky, and, water were
connected and all beings could pass freely between them.
The Raven was a trickster full of supernatural power.
He stole the sun from his grandfather, Nasshahkeeyalhl, and
made the moon and stars from it. The Raven created lakes,
rivers and filled the lands with trees. He divided night and
day, then pulled the tides into a rhythm. He filled the streams
with fresh water, scattered the eggs of salmon and trout, and
placed animals in the forests. The first human was hiding in
a giant clamshell and Raven released them onto the
beaches and gave humans fire. Raven disappeared and
took with him the power of the spirit world to communicate
and connect with humans."
    - Cheryl Samuel, University of British Columbia Press

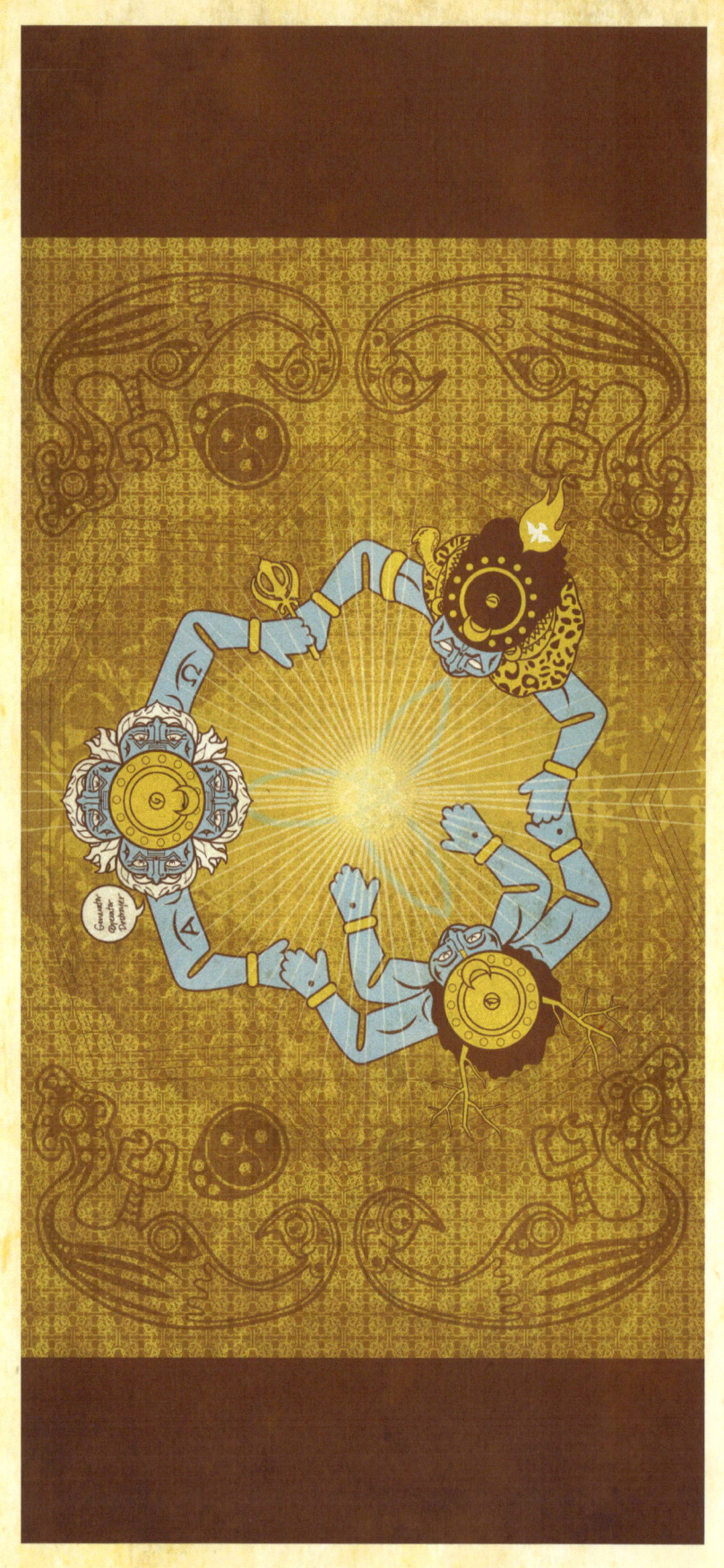

The Trinity

"When one sits in the Hoop Of The People,
one must be responsible because
All of Creation is related.
And the hurt of one is the hurt of all.
And the honor of one is the honor of all.
And whatever we do effects everything in the universe."

— White Buffalo Calf Woman

"If I thought that I was doing it myself,
the hole would close up and no power could come through.
Then everything I could do would be foolish."

— Black Elk, Oglala Sioux

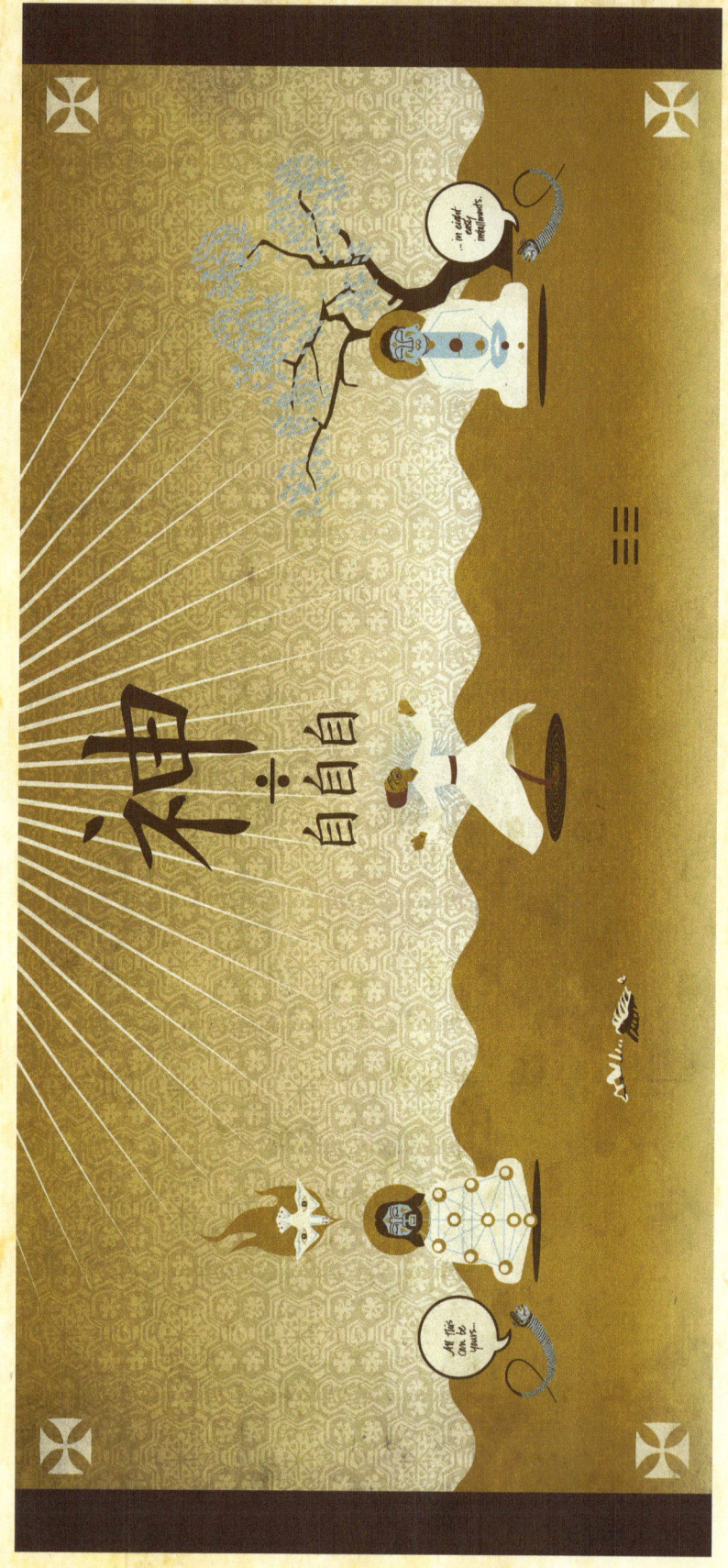

Meditation

"Go Forward With Courage

When you are in doubt, be still, and wait;

when doubt no longer exists for you, then go forward with courage.

So long as mists envelop you, be still;

be still until the sunlight pours through and dispels the mists,

as it surely will. Then act with courage."

        - White Eagle, Ponca Chief

"What you see with your eyes shut is what counts."

        - Lame Deer, Lakota

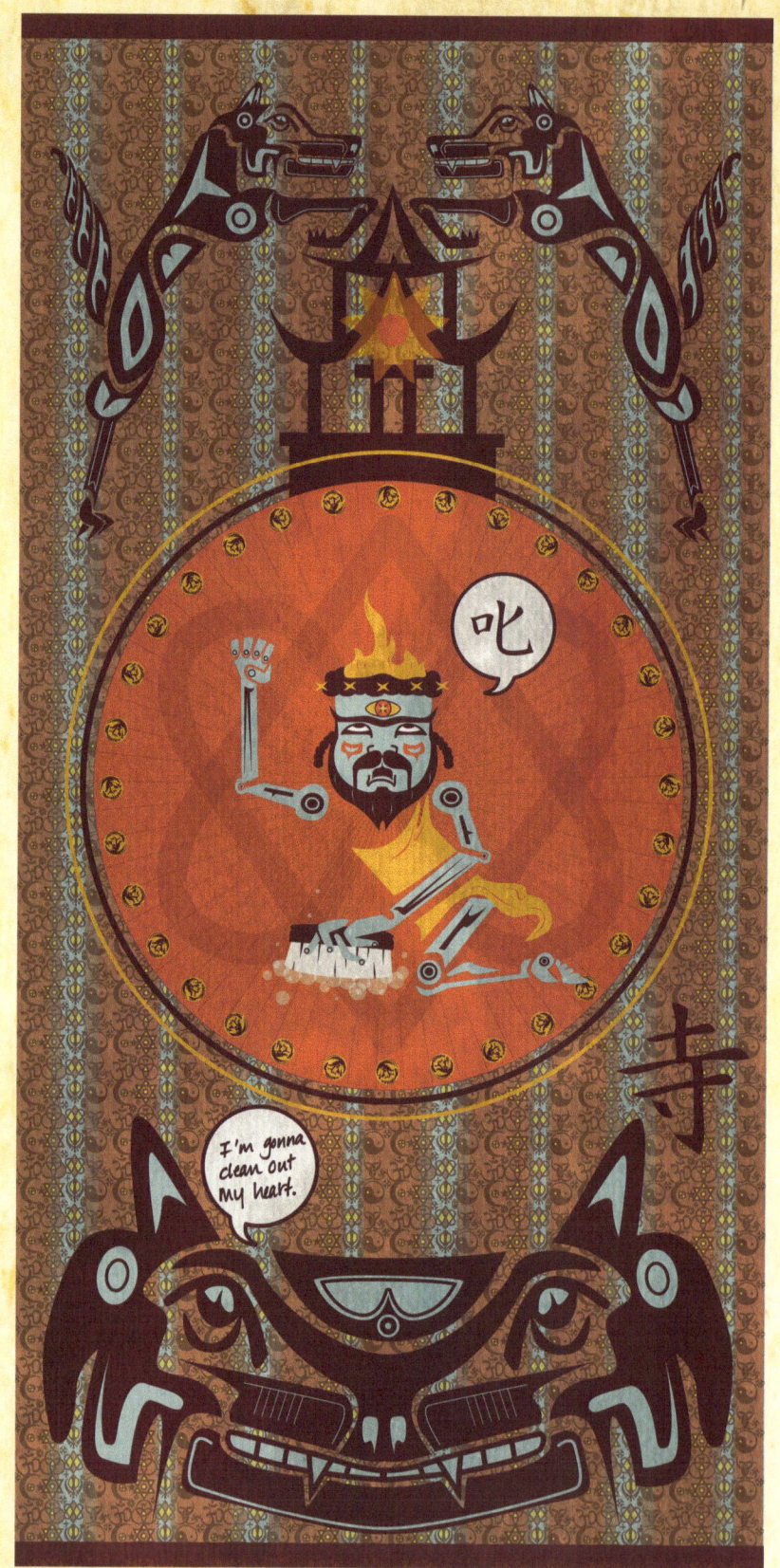

Clean The Temple

"A Native American grandfather was talking to his grandson
about how he felt. He said, 'I feel as if I have two wolves
fighting in my heart. One wolf is the vengeful, angry, violent one.
The other wolf is the loving, compassionate one.' The grandson
asked him, 'Which wolf will win the fight in your heart?'
The grandfather answered: 'The one I feed.'"
  - Native American Story

"If the Great Spirit had desired me to be a white man he
would have made me so in the first place. He put in your
heart certain wishes and plans, in my heart he put other
and different desires. Each man is good in his sight.
It is not necessary for Eagles to be Crows."
  - Sitting Bull, Hunkpapa Sioux

"If you talk to the animals they will talk with you
and you will know each other. If you do not talk to them
you will not know them, and what you do not know
you will fear. What one fears one destroys."
  - Chief Dan George

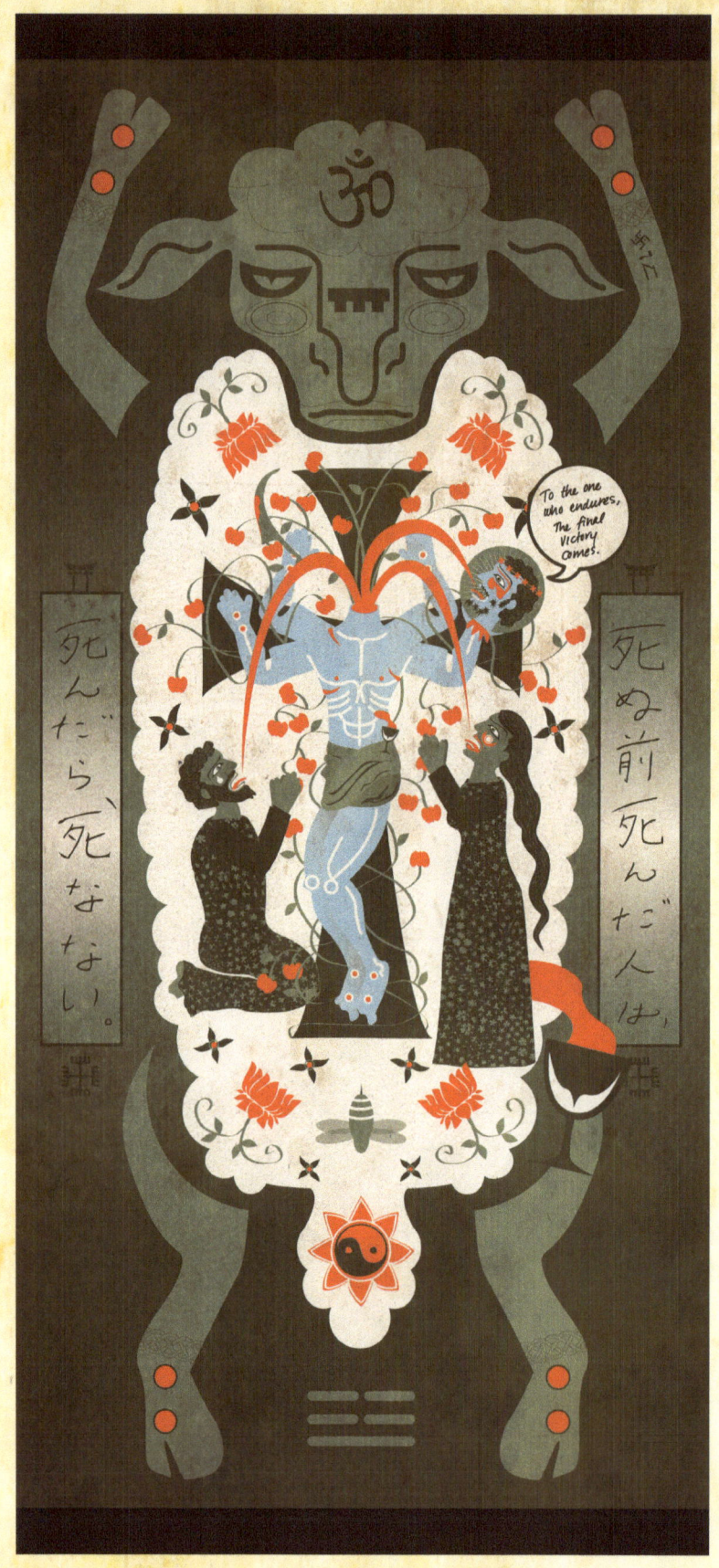

Sacrifice

"When it comes time to die, be not like those whose hearts
are filled with the fear of death, so when their time comes
they weep and pray for a little more time to live their lives
over again in a different way. Sing your death song,
and die like a hero going home."
    – Chief Tecumseh, Shawnee

Translation of Japanese text in the artwork:
He who dies before he dies, does not die when he dies.

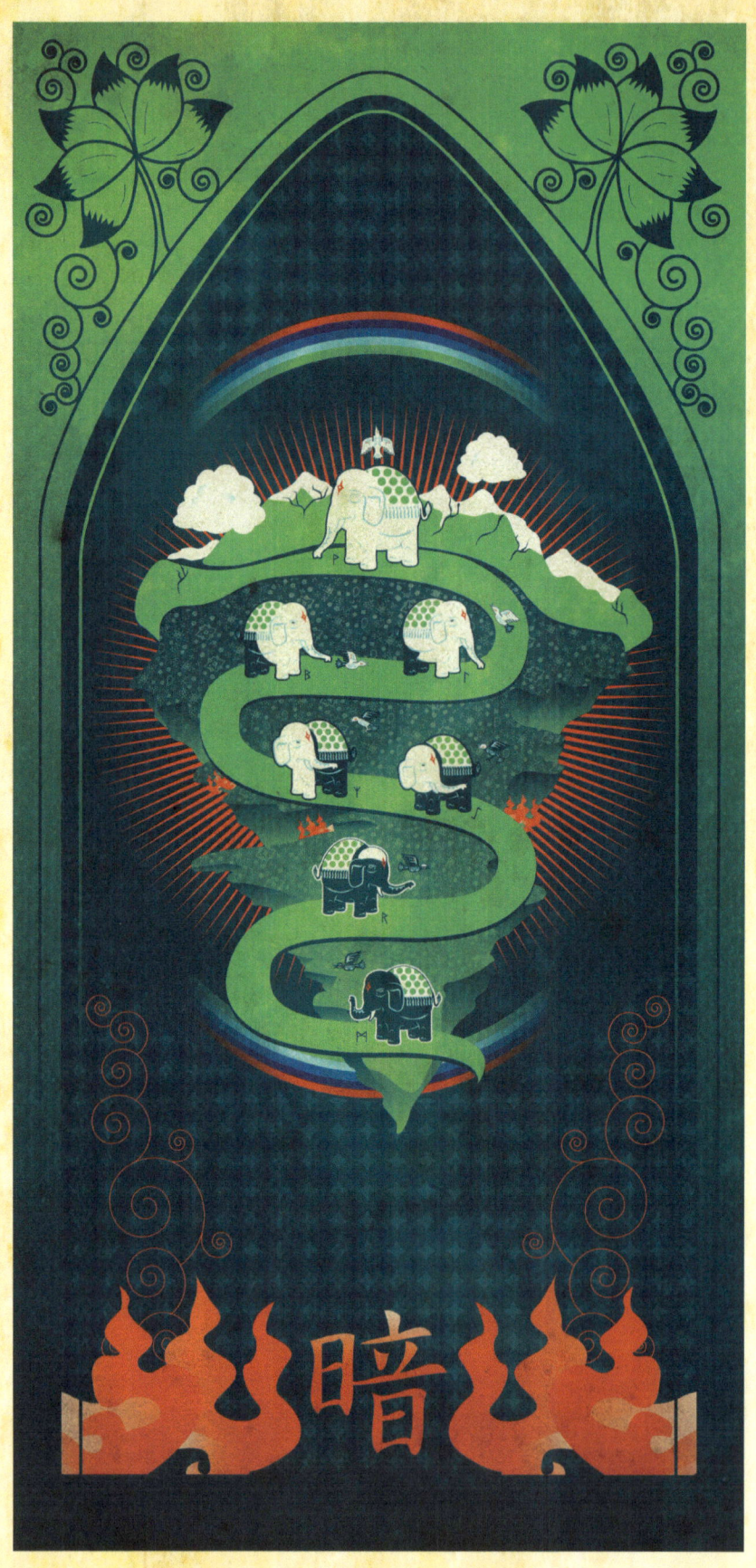

Choose A Path

"The manner with which we walk through life is each person's most important responsibility, and we should remember this with every new sunrise."
    - Thomas Yellowtail, Crow

"A vision could put you on a path you don't want to follow."
    - Lame Deer, Lakota

"It's time. If you are to walk the path of heart, then it is time..."
    - Nippawanock, Arapahoe

"He [The Great Spirit] only sketches out the path of life roughly for all the creatures on earth, shows them where to go, where to arrive, but leaves them to find their own way to get there. He wants them to act independently according to their nature, to the urges of each of them."
    - Lame Deer, Lakota

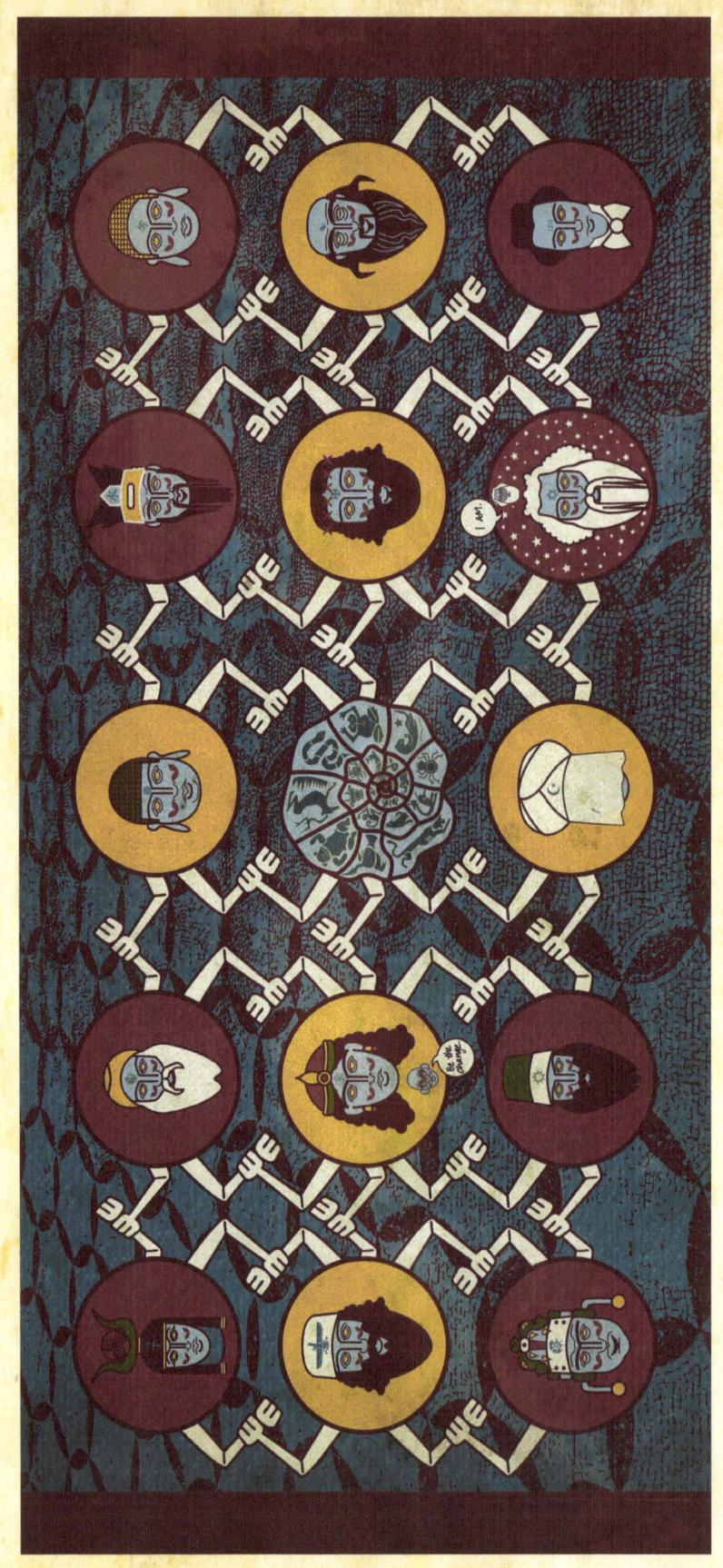

Many Paths

"The Circle has healing power. In the Circle, we are all equal. When in the Circle, no one is in front of you. No one is behind you. No one is above you. No one is below you. The Sacred Circle is designed to create unity. The Hoop of Life is also a circle. On this hoop there is a place for every species, every race, every tree and every plant. It is this completeness of Life that must be respected in order to bring about health on this planet."

~ Dave Chief, Oglala Lakota

"I was standing on the highest mountain of them all, and round about beneath me was the whole hoop of the world. And while I stood there I saw more than I can tell and I understood more than I saw; for I was seeing in a sacred manner the shapes of all things in the spirit, and the shape of all shapes as they must live together like one being. And I saw that the sacred hoop of my people was one of many hoops that made one circle, wide as daylight and as starlight, and in the center grew one mighty flowering tree to shelter all children of one mother and one father. And I saw that it was holy."

- Black Elk's Vision

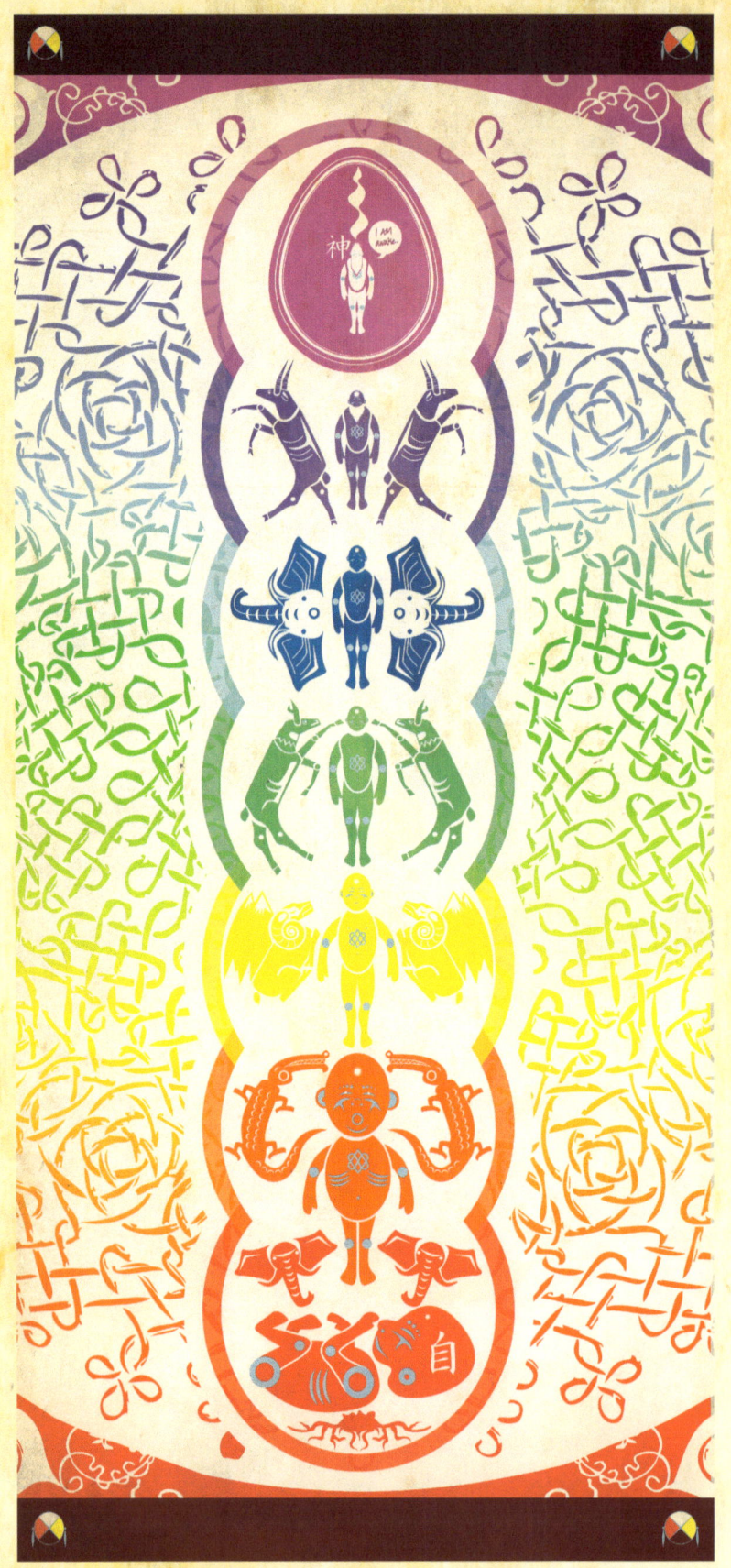

I Am

"When the Earth is sick, the animals will begin to disappear,
when that happens, The Warriors of the Rainbow will come
to save them."
    - Chief Seattle (Seatth)

"When you were born, you cried and the world rejoiced.
Live your life so that when you die,
the world cries and you rejoice."
    - White Elk

"It does not require many words to speak the truth."
    - Heinmot Tooyalaket (Chief Joseph), Nez Perce

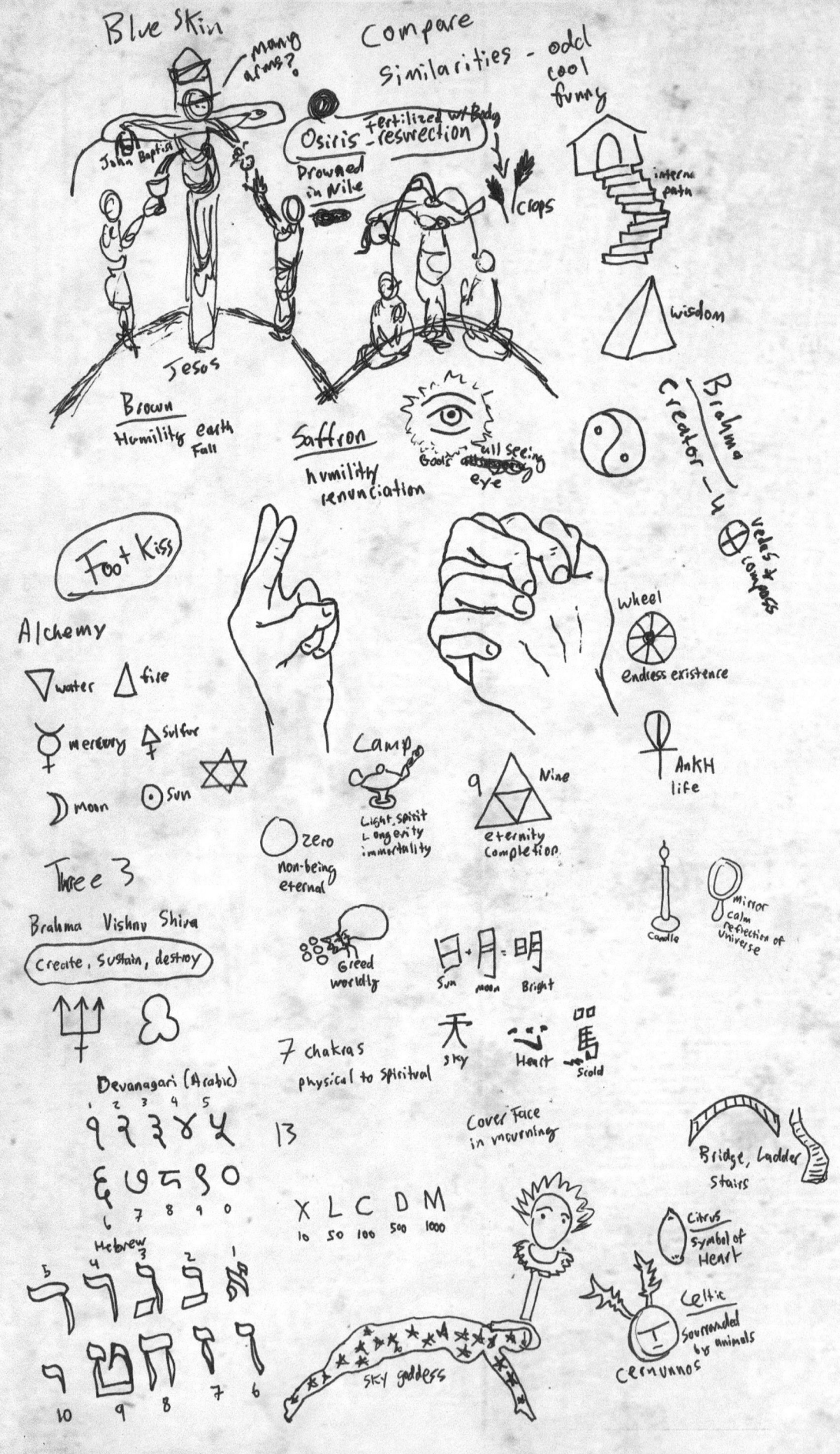

Blue Skin

Compare
Similarities - odd
cool
funny

Many arms?

John Baptist

Osiris - Fertilized w/ Body
resurrection
Drowned in Nile

crops

internal path

Jesus

wisdom

Brown
Humility earth
Fall

Saffron
humility
renunciation

Gods all seeing eye

Brahma
Creator - 4
vedas + compass

Foot Kiss

wheel
endless existence

Alchemy

▽ water   △ fire

☿ mercury   🜍 sulfur

☾ moon   ☉ Sun

AnkH life

Lamp
Light, Spirit
Longevity
immortality

Nine
eternity completion

Candle

Mirror calm reflection of Universe

○ zero
non-being
eternal

Three 3

Brahma Vishnu Shiva
Create, Sustain, destroy

Greed worldly

日 + 月 = 明
Sun moon Bright

天 sky   ♡ Heart   馬 Scold

Devanagari (Arabic)
१ २ ३ ४ ५
1 2 3 4 5

६ ७ ८ ९ ०
6 7 8 9 0

7 chakras
physical to Spiritual

13

Cover face
in mourning

Bridge, Ladder
Stairs

Hebrew

Citrus
Symbol of
Heart

Celtic
Surrounded
by animals

X L C D M
10 50 100 500 1000

10 9 8 7 6

Sky goddess

Cernunnos

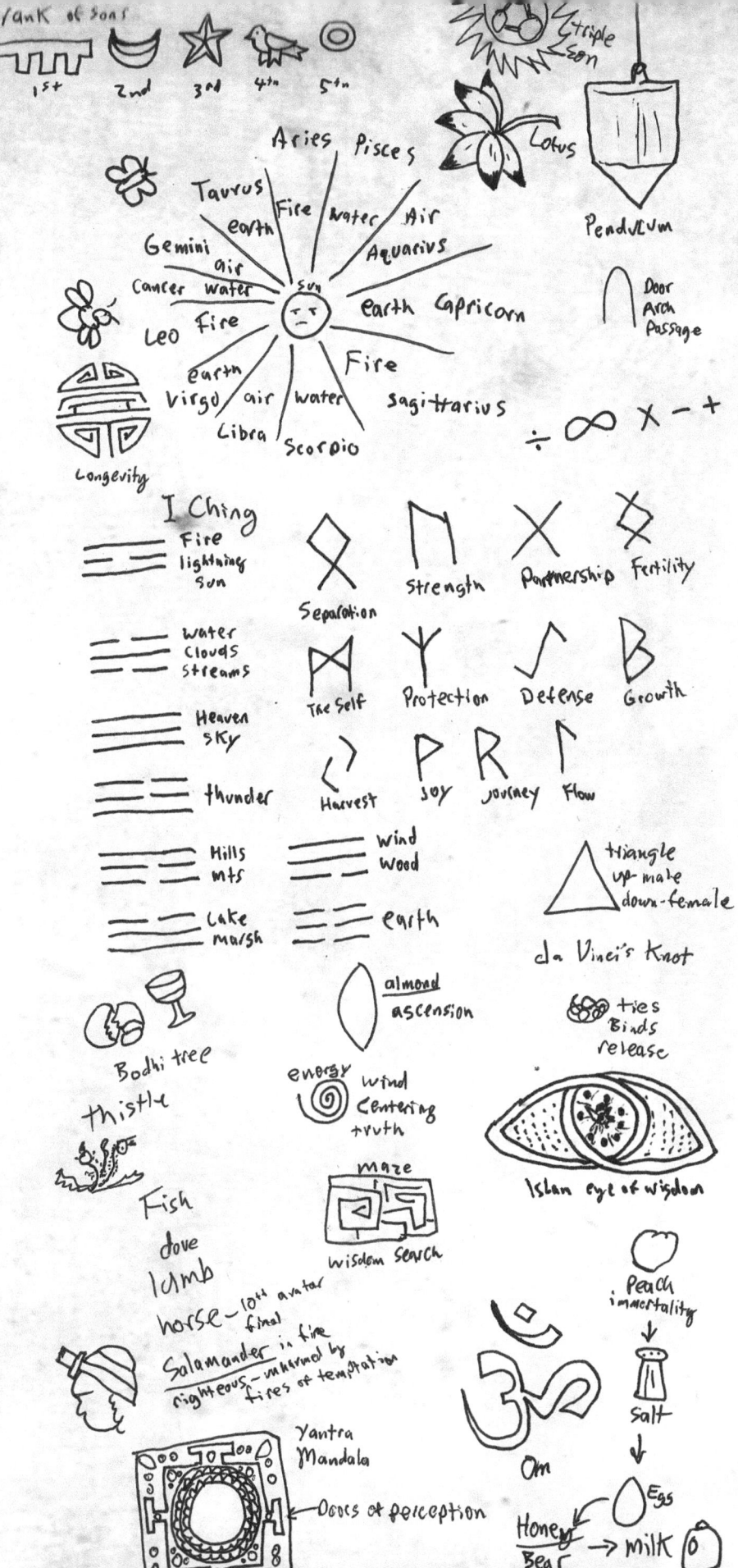

rank of sons

1st   2nd   3rd   4th   5th

Triple Son

Lotus

Pendulum

Butterfly

Aries   Pisces
Taurus
earth   Fire   water   Air
Gemini   Aquarius
air
Cancer   water   Sun   earth   Capricorn
Leo   Fire
earth   Fire
Virgo   air   water   Sagittarius
Libra
Scorpio

Door
Arch
Passage

Longevity

÷ ∞ X — +

I Ching
Fire
lightning
Sun

water
clouds
streams

Heaven
Sky

thunder

Hills
mts

Lake
marsh

Wind
Wood

earth

Separation

Strength

Partnership   Fertility

The Self   Protection   Defense   Growth

Harvest   Joy   Journey   Flow

triangle
up-male
down-female

da Vinci's Knot

almond
ascension

ties
Binds
release

Bodhi tree

thistle

energy   wind
Centering
truth

Islam eye of wisdom

maze

wisdom Search

Fish
dove
lamb
horse — 10th avatar
final
Salamander in fire
righteous — unharmed by
fires of temptation

Peach
immortality

salt

Yantra
Mandala

Om

← Doors of perception

Honey
Bear → milk

Egg

www.ingramcontent.com/pod-product-compliance
Lightning Source LLC
Chambersburg PA
CBHW060810290526

45792CB00005BA/1594